DOMINICK ARGENTO

A NATION OF COWSLIPS

Seven bagatelles for unaccompanied SATB chorus

Doggerel Verses by John Keats

BOOSEY & HAWKES

DISTRIBUTED BY

HAL•LEONARD®
CORPORATION

7777 W. BLUEMOUND RD. P.O. BOX 13819 MILWAUKEE, WI 53213

www.boosey.com
www.halleonard.com

Composer's Preface

adapted from
Catalogue Raisonné As Memoir: A Composer's Life
by Dominick Argento

Published by the University of Minnesota Press
© 2004 by Dominick Argento   Used by permission

We purchased our first home, in Minneapolis, just before I turned forty. Carolyn, my wife, had been distracted during the weeks we were house-hunting: she was getting ready to perform the role of Pamina in the Minnesota Opera's production of *The Magic Flute*. The company had employed Eleanor Steber, a renowned singer Carolyn much admired, to coach the singers. Consequently, the decision to make an offer on the house was left to me. I placed a low bid, which was relayed to the owner, who lived in California; liking the idea that I wrote music for Guthrie Theater productions, he accepted.

The house was a genuine delight to me after thirteen years of living in furnished and unfurnished apartments without a piano. My music studio on the second floor overlooked a large park and proved to be the perfect place to work. There was also a handsome Italianesque garden, all green, terraced, with a pair of stone benches, so in those first few days of occupancy in 1967, while Carolyn used the studio to practice Pamina's music, I sat in the garden and out of sheer exuberance composed in a single week of sunshine and contentment *A Nation of Cowslips* at the rate of one bagatelle a day. The poems, written in 1818, are doggerel verses that Keats had included in letters to his friends during a walking tour of England and Scotland. The gay, carefree mood of his letters and poems matched my own so perfectly that it made the composition of these a cappella pieces effortless.

The model for these seven short pieces was Hindemith's charming *Six Chansons*, a work that was highly popular with choruses and madrigal groups everywhere during my student days. By the time I was composing my set, however, Hindemith's work was being heard less often (and I don't believe I've heard it at all in the past three decades), so I hoped *Cowslips* might offer the same singing organizations a comparable substitute or replacement.

I have been told repeatedly by conductors that all my choral music is challenging or outright difficult. Yet I've been told just as often by the choristers themselves that they enjoy singing it. I like to think my choral parts are generally considerate of the singers: the individual lines themselves are never awkward; care is taken to provide reference points for finding entrance pitches; very few demands are made regarding stamina or range.

CONTENTS

A NATION OF COWSLIPS

for Winifred Baker

1. THE DEVON MAID

JOHN KEATS

DOMINICK ARGENTO

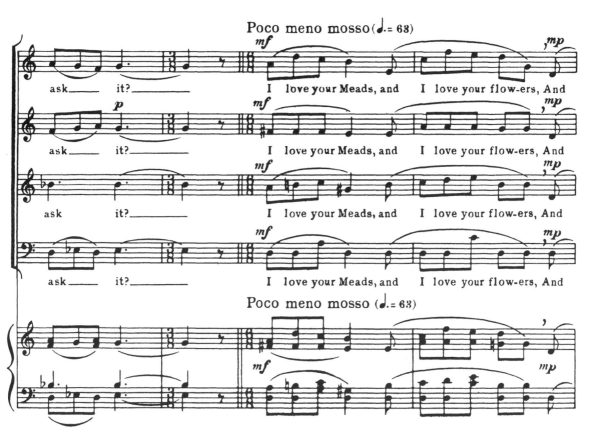

6

Molto meno mosso (♩.=56)

I love your hills,— and I love your dales,— And I love your flocks a-

Tempo I

-bleat-ing But O, on the heath-er to lie to- geth-er,—

for Peter DeLone

2. ON VISITING OXFORD

JOHN KEATS   DOMINICK ARGENTO

* Stagger breathing: phrases should be unbroken. Dotted barlines indicate only the co-ordination of high and low voices, not accents.

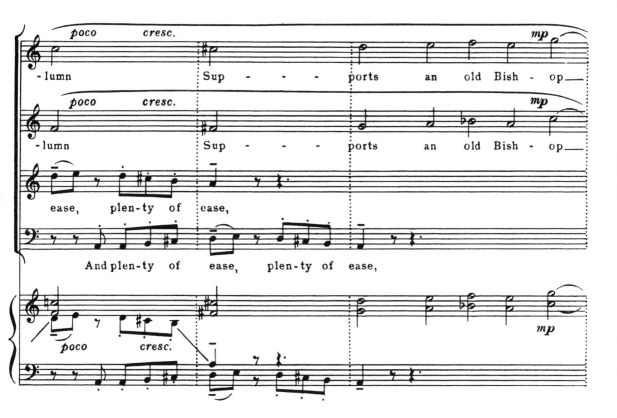

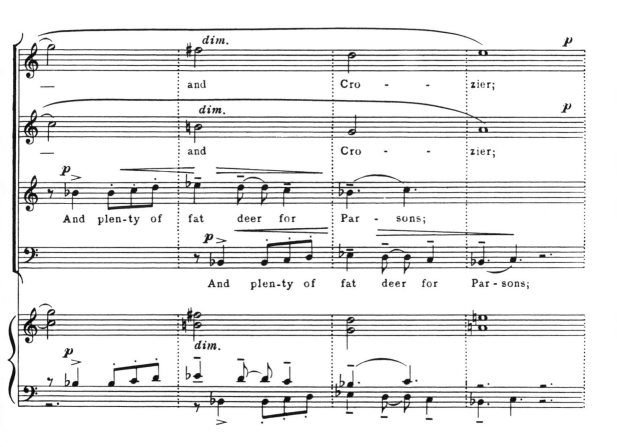

12

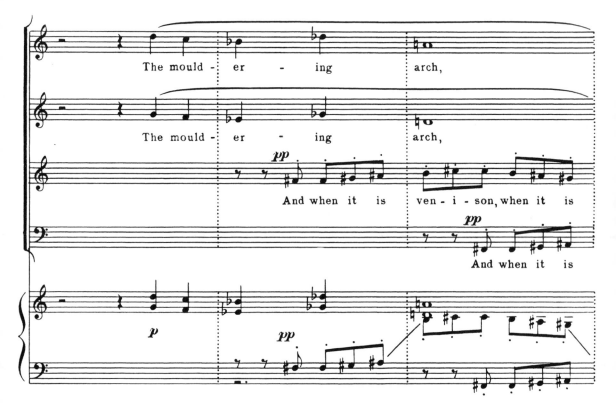

14

Stesso tempo

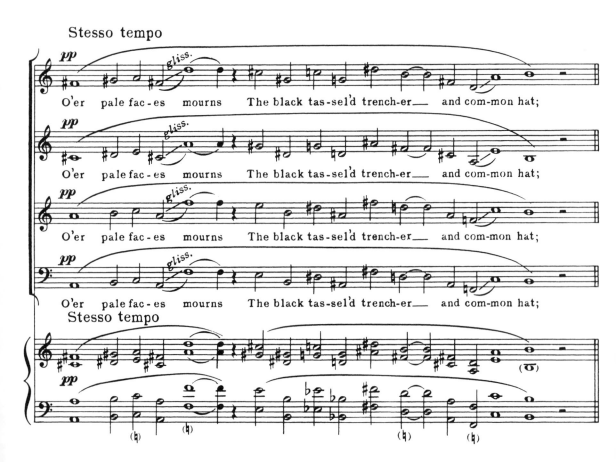

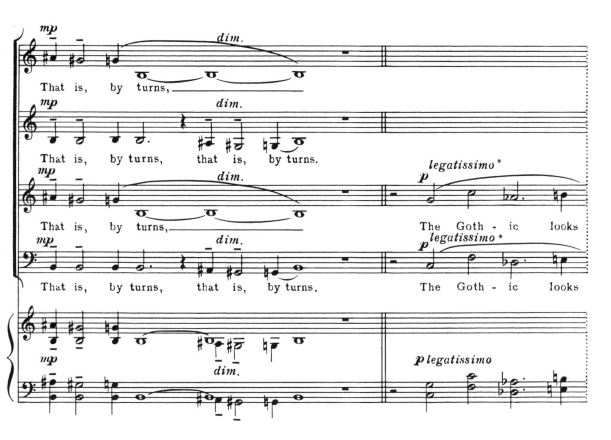

* Stagger breathing: phrases should be unbroken.

16

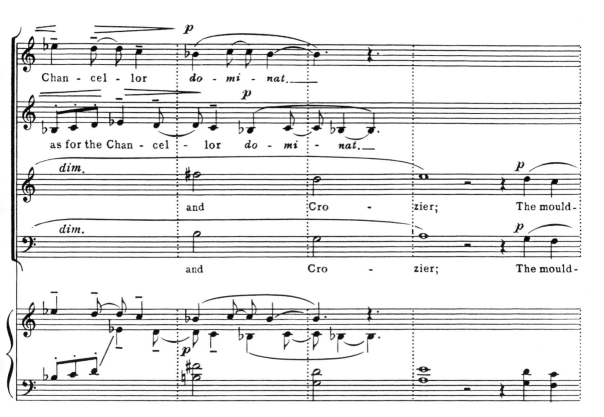

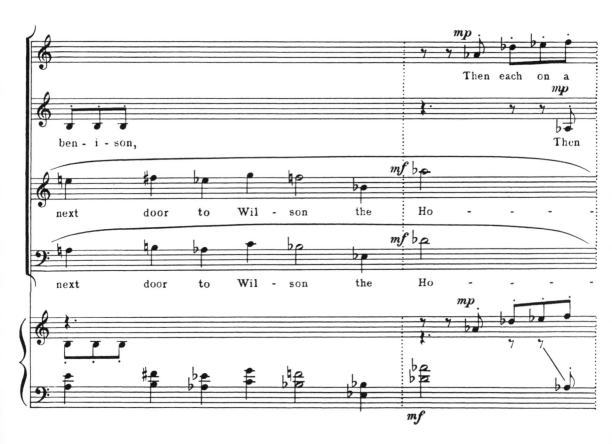

for Charles Schwartz

3. SHARING EVE'S APPLE

JOHN KEATS

DOMINICK ARGENTO

22

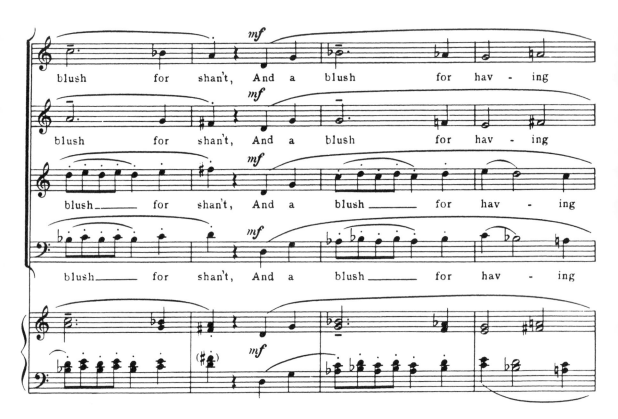

26

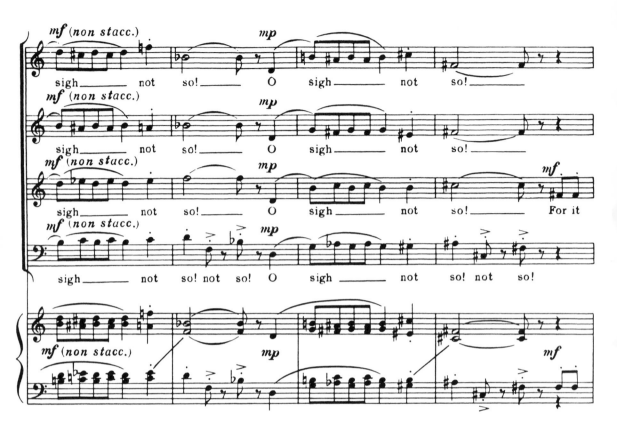

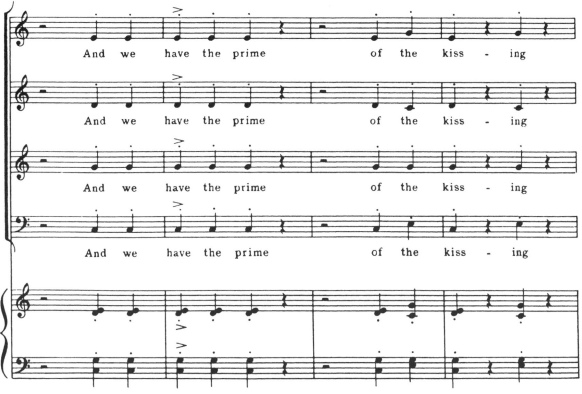

30

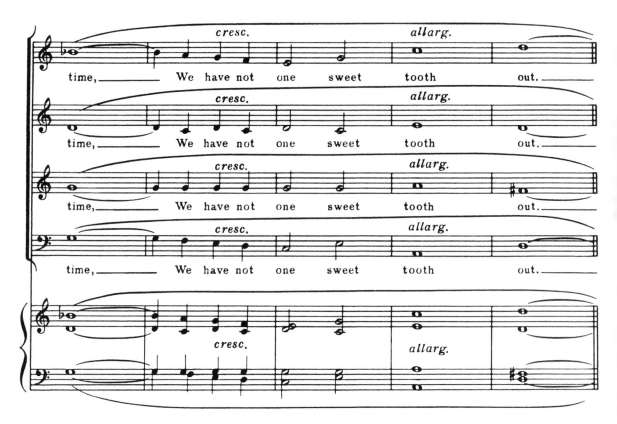

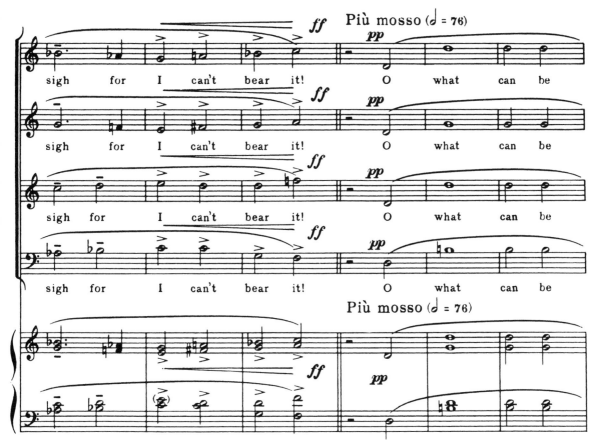

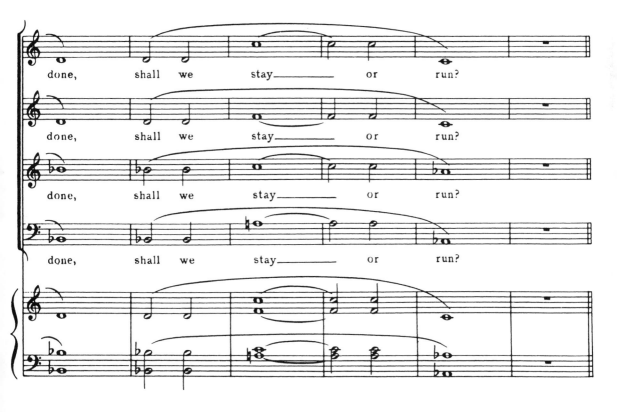

32

(This page intentionally left blank to facilitate page turns.)

34

for Frederic Hilary

4. THERE WAS A NAUGHTY BOY

JOHN KEATS

DOMINICK ARGENTO

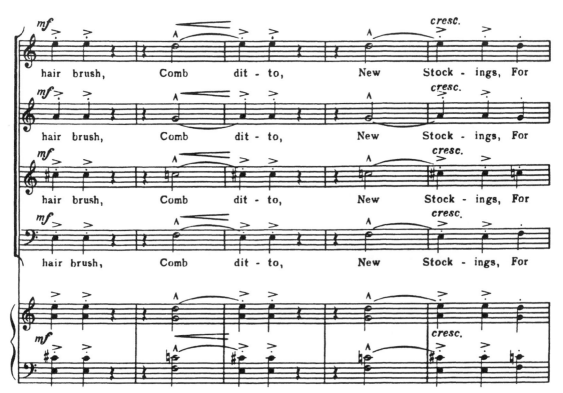

hair brush, Comb dit - to, New Stock - ings, For

hair brush, Comb dit - to, New Stock - ings, For

hair brush, Comb dit - to, New Stock - ings, For

hair brush, Comb dit - to, New Stock - ings, For

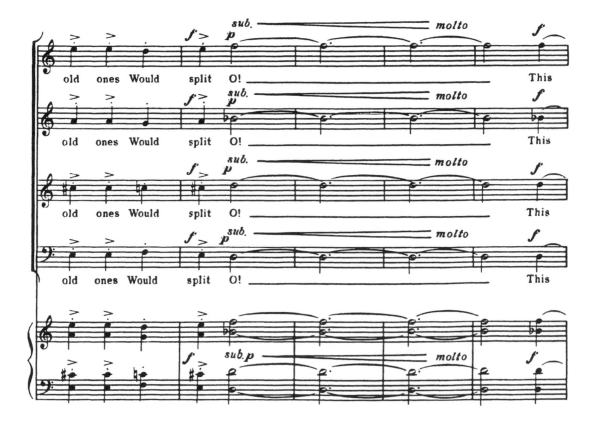

old ones Would split O! _____ This

old ones Would split O! _____ This

old ones Would split O! _____ This

old ones Would split O! _____ This

* Tenors and basses may exchange parts.

40

Subito molto espansivo

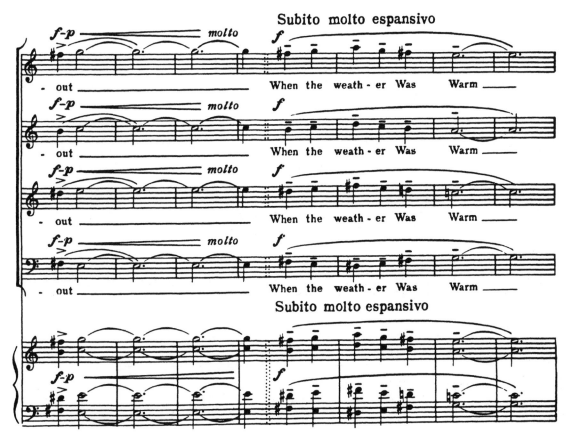

42

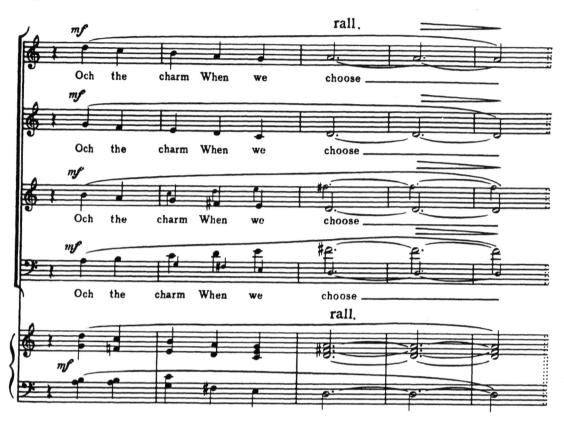

Come Prima

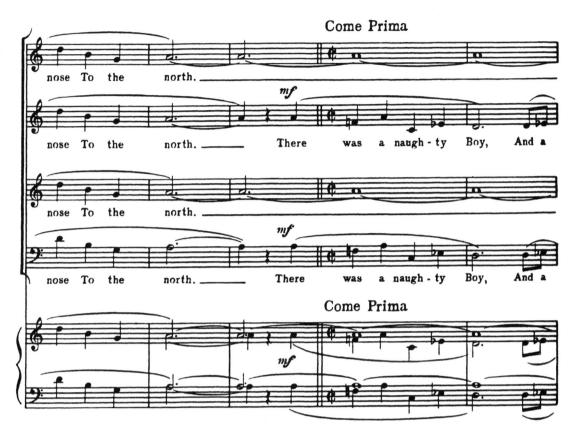

Come Prima

44

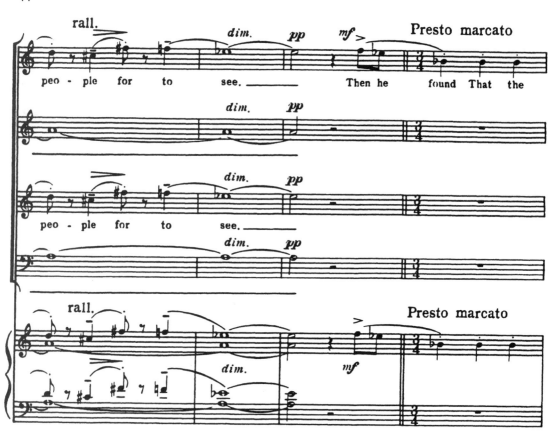

46

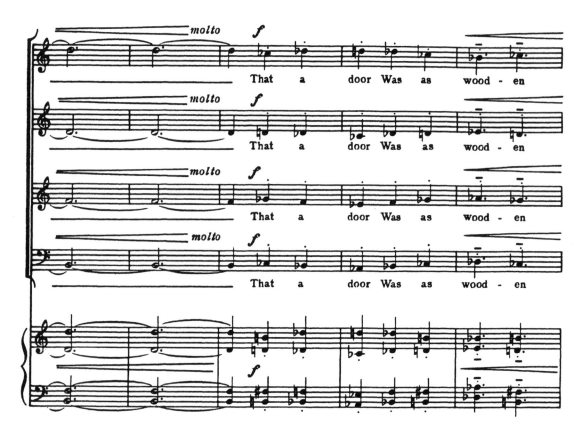

(This page intentionally left blank to facilitate page turns.)

for Donald Aird

5. A PARTY OF LOVERS AT TEA

JOHN KEATS

DOMINICK ARGENTO

else for-get the pur-pose of the night, For-get their

else for-get the pur-pose of the night, For-get their

else for-get the pur-pose of the night, For-get their

else for-get the pur-pose of the night, For-get their

tea, for-get their ap - pe - tite. See with

tea, for-get their ap - pe - tite. See with

tea, for-get their ap - pe - tite. See with

tea, for-get their ap - pe - tite.

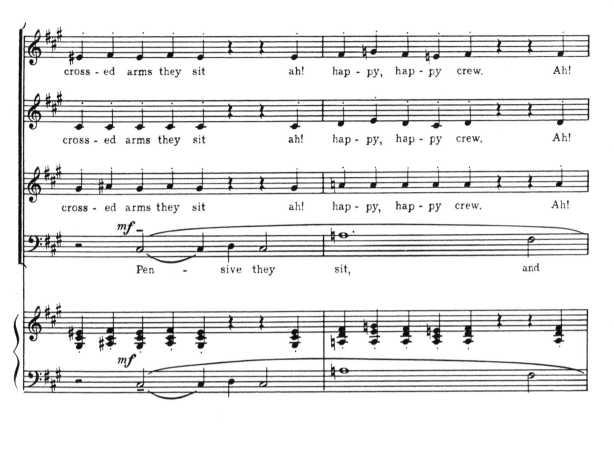

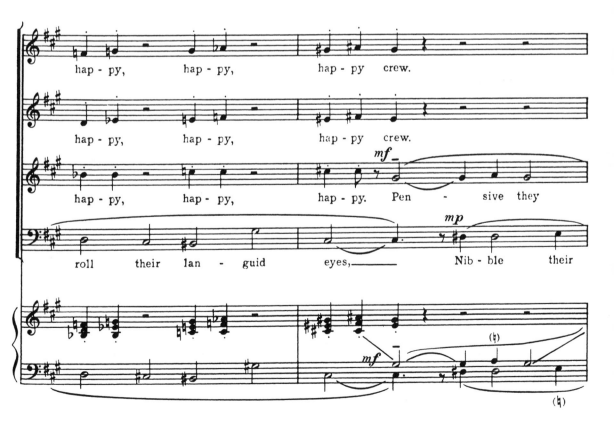

52

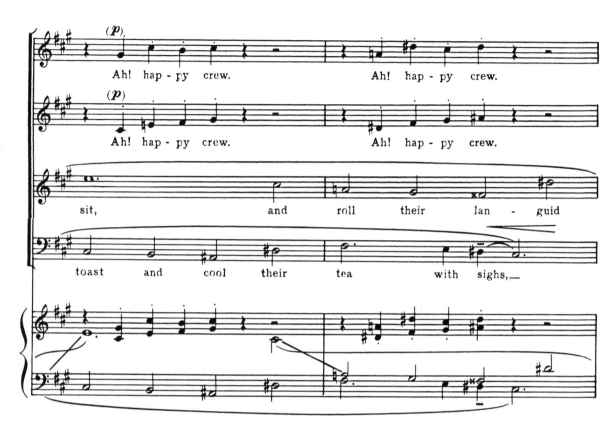

hap - py crew. Pen - sive they
roll their lan - guid eyes, Nib - ble their
tea with sighs, sighs Or else for -
of the night, For - get the tea, for -

sit, and roll their lan - guid eyes, Nib - ble their
toast and cool their tea with sighs, sighs, Or else for -
get the pur - pose of the night, For - get their tea, for -
get their ap - pe - tite. See with cross-ed arms they

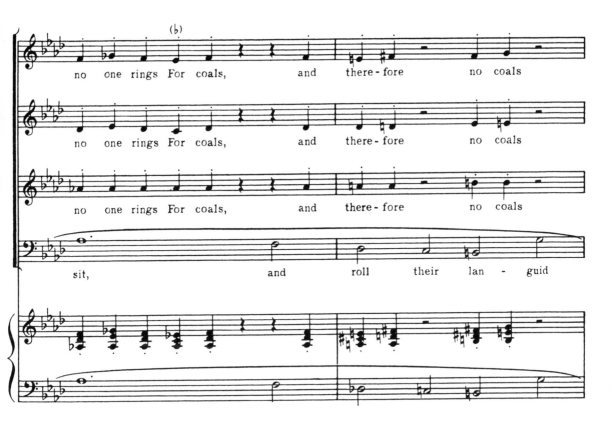

must he die By a hu - mane so - ci - e - ty?*

must he die By a hu - mane so - ci - e - ty?*

must he die By a hu - mane so - ci - e - ty?*

tea with sighs,— sighs,— Or else for -

No, No; there Mis - ter Wer - ter takes his spoon, In-serts it,

No, No; there Mis - ter Wer - ter takes his spoon, In-serts it,

No, No; there Mis - ter Wer - ter takes his spoon, In-serts it,

- get the pur - pose of the night, For -

* Rhyme with 'die'.

58

Come prima (♩ = 56)
p mezzo voce

mark. Yet... Pen - sive they sit, and roll their lan-guid
mark. Yet... Pen - sive they sit, and roll their lan-guid
mark. Yet... Pen - sive they sit, and roll their lan-guid
tea. Yet... Pen - sive they sit, and roll their lan-guid

Come prima (♩ = 56)

* (SOLO TENOR)
A - las, my friend! your coat sits ve-ry well;

* (SOLO BASS)
Ah me! I must a - way.

eyes, Nib - ble their toast, and
eyes, Nib - ble their toast, and
eyes, Nib - ble their toast, and
eyes, Nib - ble their toast, and

* Spoken rather freely: the notation of rhythm merely suggests the relationship between this exchange and the chorus.

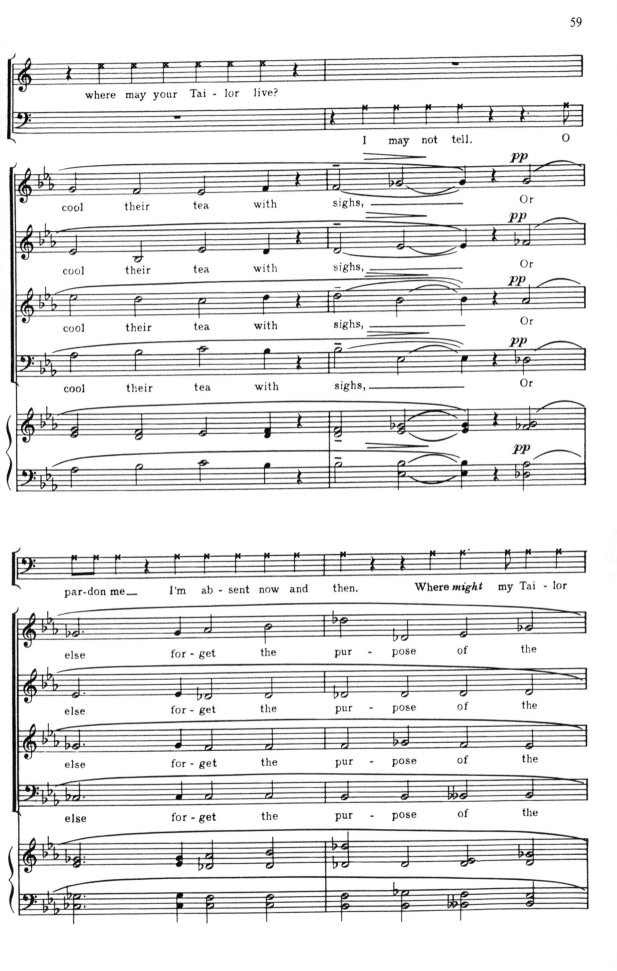

62

for Larry Fleming

6. TWO OR THREE POSIES

JOHN KEATS

DOMINICK ARGENTO

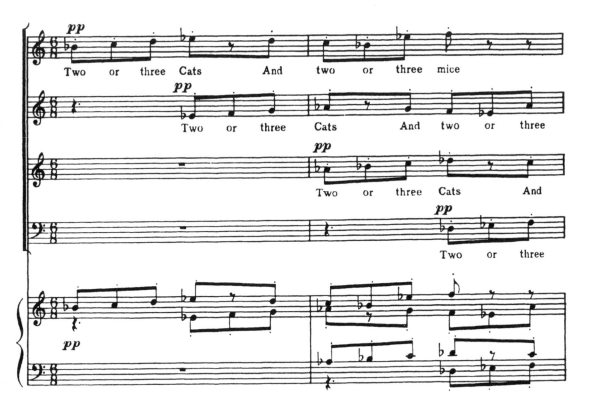

Quasi adagio (♩. = 56)

Two or three san - dies And two or three tab - bies

Two or three san - dies And two or three tab - bies

Two or three san - dies And two or three tab - bies

Two or three san - dies And two or three tab - bies

Quasi adagio (♩. = 56)

Two or three dan - dies And two Miss - us mum! _____
(bocca chiusa)

Two or three dan - dies And two Miss - us mum! _____
(bocca chiusa)

Two or three dan - dies And two Miss - us mum! _____
(bocca chiusa)

Two or three dan - dies And two Miss - us mum! _____
(bocca chiusa)

Tempo I

Two or three Smiles And two or three frowns _____

Two or three Smiles And two or three frowns _____

Two or three Smiles And two or three frowns _____

Two or three Smiles And two or three frowns _____

Tempo I

Two or three Miles To two or three towns _____ Two or three pegs _____

Two or three Miles To two or three towns _____ Two or three pegs _____

Two or three Miles To two or three towns _____ Two or three pegs _____

Two or three Miles To two or three towns _____ Two or three pegs _____

68

(This page intentionally left blank to facilitate page turns.)

for Earl George

7. IN PRAISE OF APOLLO

JOHN KEATS

DOMINICK ARGENTO

* All accents (>) very marked.

72

* ᴧ = Upper neighbor:

fol - low, I fol - - low, I fol - low:__ Hence,

fol - low, I fol - - low, I fol - low:__ Hence,

I fol - low, I fol - low, I fol - low:__ O,__ my

I fol - low, I fol - low:__ O,__ my

Bur-gun-dy, Clar-et, and Port, A - way with old Hock and Ma-dei-ra, Too

Bur-gun-dy, Clar-et, and Port, A - way with old Hock and Ma-dei-ra, Too

bowl is the sky, And_ I drink at my eye

bowl is the sky, And_ I drink at my eye

earth-ly ye are for my sport; There's a bev - er - age bright - er

earth-ly ye are for my sport; There's a bev - er - age bright - er

Till ___ I feel ___ in the brain ___ A Del -

Till ___ I feel ___ in the brain ___ A Del -

and clear - er. Hence, and clear - er.

and clear - er. Hence, and clear - er.

- phian pain ___ O, ___ my -phian pain ___ On the

- phian pain ___ O, ___ my -phian pain ___ On the

green of the hill We will drink our fill Of gold-en sun-shine,__

green of the hill We will drink our fill Of gold-en sun-shine,__

On the green of the

On the green of the

__ Till our brains in-ter-twine.__ O,__ my bowl is the

__ Till our brains in-ter-twine.__ O,__ my bowl is the

* ⁀ = Lower neighbor:

78

fol - low:___ With the glo - ry and grace of A -

fol - low:___ With the glo - ry and grace of A -

fol - low:___ With the glo - ry and grace of A -

fol - low:___ With the glo - ry and grace of A -

- pol - lo! The God of Song, the God___ of Song! With the

- pol - lo! The God of Song, the God___ of Song! With the

- pol - lo! The God of Song, the God___ of Song! O,___ my

- pol - lo! The God of Song, the God___ of Song! O,___ my

Till _____ I feel _____ in the gold - en sun - shine, _____

earth - ly ye are for my sport; There's a - pol - lo, The

brain _____ A Del - phian pain _____ With the Till our brains in - ter - twine. _____ Hence, bev - er - age bright - er and clear - er. On the God of Song! the God _____ of Song! O, _____ my

Subito meno mosso (♩ = 112 ca)

86